We are All Socialists Now

A Deplorable looks at the 2020 *Election*

Charles Moscowitz

Table of Contents

Opening Thoughts

The 2020 election was stolen from President Donald J. Trump who won the election in a landslide. I will reflect upon the facts and the nature of that theft and I will analyze the potential ramifications to our country by asking weather America has now, as a result of that theft, effectively become a Socialist state. Certainly, while the Joe Biden regime will no doubt attempt to implement a socialistic agenda, the problems associated with the leftward tilt that his installation as president represents holds deeper sociological ramifications. Those of us who are part of what I would describe as a growing American populist movement, one that President Trump so boldly defined and one that he so valiantly spearheaded, will defend our civil rights by resistance and by a non-violent opposition to this anti-American trend.

During the election of 2020, by far the most corrupt in American history, we witnessed unprecedented levels of officially sanctioned and coordinated ballot fraud that was often carried out in the open. The corruption that overtook our election and, more broadly, that overtook our system of government in general turned out to be much more ingrained than we had imagined it would be. We have witnessed the means by which the controlling establishments of both political parties, the media, the so-called independent judiciary on both on the state and the federal level, state governments, major institutions of culture, business, academia, and even many of our churches conspired, at various levels both consciously and otherwise, to coordinate and to concertize the stealing of the election and the denouncement, communist style, of Donald Trump and of the movement that he represents.

But the problem is even more fundamental than that.

We have witnessed the fact that a significant percentage of our fellow citizens either do not seem to care, or they are willfully ignorant of the facts, or worse, that they are fully conscious witting participants in the election theft of 2020. Those who generally do not care were mostly rendered docile by a four-year steady diet of nonstop propaganda and lies told about Donald Trump and his Administration which had been, by any objective standard, one of the most successful in American history.

Those who were witting and conscious participants in the conspiracy to overthrow the election were largely motivated by an agenda that sought to stop Trump and to stop, as such, the advance of a genuinely progressive political and cultural movement that seeks to put America first. Those who were consciously and wittingly involved in this conspiracy were either disloyal internationalists who sought to turn America into a petty province of the world or they were mentally deficient utopians who tend to believe that such freedom fostering institutions as sovereignty, property, individual rights and other various democratic principles are anachronisms and superstitions that represent a bygone era to be denigrated and eventually discarded.

It is particularly troubling to witness so many young college age Americans becoming part of the mob that the conspirators have deliberately generated over time. Perhaps many of the millennials have been subtly but effectively brainwashed by the system of public education and by a culture that pushes a Marxist woke agenda. Many of our young people seem to have no idea who they are let alone what the American political philosophy is.

Perhaps, as a society, we have reached a point of critical mass in terms of succumbing to a vast and advancing socialist conspiracy that finds its modern roots in the election of Woodrow Wilson, the first self-described Socialist, as President of the United States in the pivotal year 1912.

The sad and troubling fact is every American knows, at least they know it in their heart of hearts, and while this does not include someone who might have just crawled out from under a rock, that the 2020 election was stolen.

Perhaps, as a nation and as a society, we have reached a point of no return.

The Cause

Is there really any doubt over the demonstrable fact that President Donald J. Trump, the 45th President of the United States, had to face a concerted and coordinated conspiracy meant to tarnish both his reptation and that of his movement from the moment that he and the future First Lady Melania Trump stepped off the elevator at Trump Tower in Manhattan where he announced his candidacy for the presidency on June 15th, 2015? Is there really any question regarding the subsequent launching of a relentless conspiracy to remove him from office, or to damage his functional ability and diminish his influence once he was inaugurated as President of the United States on January 20th, 2017? at least severely

In our free country, political criticism is not only normal and expected but it is rightfully encouraged. American traditions indicate that such criticism, both on the policy level as well as on the personal level in terms of criticism of our leaders and those who hold positions of influence, including engaging in reasonable degrees of mockery and scorn, are assumed to be the normal functioning of a free people. The attack against President Trump was not, however, normal as it was not conducted in the spirit of a loyal opposition that held the best interests of the country at heart or the maintenance of the fabric of our society in mind. The nature of the attack against Trump, the unmasking, the spying, the sleepers embedded into the White House by Obama on his way out, the investigations, the perjury traps, the phony impeachments, the lies and the deceptions carried out with alacrity and vigor by the fake news media, all of this has been well chronicled elsewhere.

For the conspirators, President Trump represented a real and present threat to both their power and their wealth, as his enemies clearly included most of the top 1% wealthiest people in America and around the world, but, more fundamentally, his presidency threatened their world view, one that had been enthroned and one that had wormed its way into the lofty places of power over a hundred-year period.

Trump threated to undo a century of creeping Socialism, what Trump advisor Steve Bannon called the administrative state, and in the process, Trump threatened to wake up the sleeping beast of the average working citizen.

Every modern president had given lip service to such things as securing the national border from the incursion of illegal aliens, being tough on crime, holding the line on taxes, getting rid of onerous regulation, reducing the foreign trade deficit, standing up to the Russkies, the Islamic terrorists, the Chi-Coms, reducing unemployment and standing up for the working man and woman. For President Trump, these commitments represented more than mere rhetoric and more than the usual blather and bumper-sticker sloganeering.

When it came to these issues Donald Trump meant business and, in the process, he exposed the lies and the deceptions of the establishment. Trump is a brash and plain-spoken independent businessman who is not afraid to fight for what he believes in and he is not, as such, beholden to any special interests. The things that Trump stands for are well known, consistent, and have been well articulated by him over several decades of public life. Trump's independence and his personal wealth, which meant that unlike the Clintons, Barack Obama, Joe Biden and many other politicians from both political parties, he would not use his political office to enrich himself. This meant that Trump could not be controlled by any person or by any group. Trump, who lost money as president, was thus virtually incorruptible and this factor, more than anything else, threatened the establishment. Unlike most politicians, especially those who hold high office, Trump could not be blackmailed.

The snobbish elitist eastern seaboard liberal establishment, with their aristocratic pretensions and their phony British accents, have long employed the style and verbiage of what French scholar Alain Benascon called totalitarian language. They talk down their noses to the rest of us mere mortals. They assume the position of Moses descending from Sinai each day to deliver to us peons the supreme gift of their enlightened opinions. Those of us who would aspire to benefit from the many riches that this establishment subtly lords over our heads learn how to imitate and how to emulate their effete mannerisms from our classrooms, from Hollywood movies, from their media mandarins, and from the millions of memes and images that they relentlessly saturate us with each and every day. We get the message that we are rewarded handsomely with social acceptance for accepting their version of reality and we likewise come to understand that we are punished, in no uncertain terms, for any hint of rejection on our part. We internalize all of this and we learn, somewhere down the line, to keep our heads low.

Then along comes Donald Trump wielding his big stick which he shoves into their perfectly formed beehive. Trump has released the sound and the fury of an Exorcist like raging cloud of a thousand buzzing bees.

The run-up to the 2020 Election

The year 2020 started out on a strange and discordant note.

The previous year had witnessed the collapse of the Mueller probe, a three-year fishing expedition that had sought to prove the strangest conspiracy theory of modern times which was that Donald Trump had been spying for Russia. The run-up to that bizarre episode began even before his election when the 2016 presidential campaign of Hillary Clinton, using Russian sources, had concocted a dossier on Trump that was meant to prove that he was, essentially, a Russian asset. The compliant mainstream media worked hand in glove with what would evolve into a clique of conspirators and supporting apparatchiks who would launch a feeding frenzy that included the virtual obliteration of what had previously been journalistic standards in their zeal to bring Trump down. The mainstream media would proceed to routinely run stories up the proverbial flagpole that were not sourced, stories that would emanate from one anonymous source or were derived from illegal phone wiretaps. The scam would then be completed when the bogus stories would be retracted, usually the next day and in small print, after the damage was done.

The discredited dossier, known as the pee dossier, was used by FBI Director James Comey, who had previously let Hillary Clinton off the hook for trucking in top-secret emails and for destroying others that had been subpoenaed by the FBI, in order to get permission from the FISA court to spy on minor Trump advisor Carter Page and this effectively opened the door to spying on the Trump campaign and then on the Trump presidency. When President Trump legally and appropriately fired Comey, this was somehow used as an excuse by assistant Attorney General Rod Rosenstein to appoint former FBI Director Robert Mueller as Special Council.

The history of this attempted coup de etat is beyond the scope of this brief treatise as this has been well and extensively covered elsewhere. Suffice to say that the deep state, as President Trump has so accurately called it, worked feverishly over the first three years of his presidency to harass him and to stymie his administration and the agenda that he was elected to enact at every turn. We should note that a cumulative consequence of the actions of the deep state in this regard, emboldened as they were by their close allies as well as their collaborators in the media, including the increasingly censorious big tech social media, was a significant erosion of our civil liberties. It would now become ok, in a context fueled by this inchoate drumbeat of Trump hatred, to bug phones, spy on people, arrest harmless elderly citizens with swat teams and the media parked outside on their lawns, and with prosecutors and judges pushing for long prison terms for minor process crimes.

The election year 2020 began with the phony impeachment of President Trump, an event that has since slipped down the proverbial memory hole, on charges that no one really remembers. In a nutshell, Trump had asked the newly elected Ukrainian President Volodymyr Zelensky to look into whether or not Vice President Biden had used the political influence of his office to help strike a sweetheart deal for his son Hunter Biden with the Ukrainian Burisma Oil Company which was at that time under criminal investigation. It has since been confirmed that Hunter made a deal with Burisma that paid him at least $50 thousand dollars a month and that Vice President Biden had boasted, during a televised conversation at an event that was sponsored by the Council on Foreign Relations, that he had threatened to hold up financial aid to Ukraine unless the Ukrainian government fired a special prosecutor, Viktor Shokin, who was at that time investigating potential corruption at Burisma, an investigation that might have exposed Hunter Biden.

The basis for the impeachment charge was the allegation that President Trump had asked the Ukrainian President to concoct evidence against Biden in order to hurt him as a potential opponent in the upcoming election. Yet the Hunter Biden scandal, which would later extend to shady business dealings with Russian oligarchs and Chinese corporations, and the level of support that those deals received from the sitting Vice President, was well documented and common knowledge that had been reported in the media at the time. President Trump, or any American president, would be acting within their appropriate purview to ask any world leader, in this case the President of Ukraine, to investigate any form of corruption that might have involved any American citizen or company. Furthermore, it would have been perfectly appropriate for Trump to delay congressionally approved foreign aid to any nation that refused to aid in any such investigation. Indeed, this was exactly what Vice President Biden had himself threatened to do, but in his case his threat was self-serving and, as such, his threat was for all the wrong reasons.

So, first we started the year 2020 off with the phony impeachment in January and then, by late February, we had the COVID-19 worldwide pandemic. The initial executive action taken by President Trump in response to COVID was to ban airline flights from China for non-citizens. China had been identified by the slow-moving World Health Organization as at the epicenter of the virus. The predictable response on the part of the anti-Trump conspirators, which would be buttressed by the conditioned knee-jerk reaction on the part of the media, was to screech that this move was proof that Trump had something against Chinese people. This piece of propaganda neatly fit into the big lie they had been pushed, as an article of faith, from day one which was that Donald Trump, and, by extension, his movement had something against people of color who are, I note, Trump's natural constituency.

The initial reaction to the pandemic on the part of Democratic leaders such as Nancy Pelosi, as well as some Republicans, was to ignore the threat. Pelosi, in an event that was televised, urged people in late February to come on down to Chinatown in San Francisco, to go to parades and to go to Chinatown restaurants as a political act of defiance against a president who she implied was fear-mongering around the pandemic. A reasonable criticism could, in retrospect, be lodged against both the President and Republican as well as Democratic leaders in terms of their slow response to the threat the virus posed and, while history tends to hold 20-20 vision and while history is to be understood in the context of confirmation bias, including that of this author, nevertheless there is plenty of blame to go around.

How, then, did COVID affect the 2020 election?

In general, the emergency atmosphere that accompanied the advent of COVID contributed to an expansion of fiat governing powers which would be assumed by various state governors, particularly the governors of the so-called blue states like New York, New Jersey, Michigan and California. These powers would permit, for example, Governor Gretchen Witmer of Michigan to enforce arbitrary regulations such as those which would permit the purchase of booze and lottery tickets while banning the purchase of planting seeds and gardening appliances. More darkly, such assumed powers would be used by New York Governor Andrew Cuomo to bypass federal regulations by placing COVID active patients into nursing homes thus exposing the most vulnerable segment of our population to this dread disease. This led to the deaths of unknown tens of thousands of people as, according to the Center for Disease Control, over 50% of the known deaths from COVID were within the population range of over 80 years old. These powers assumed by governors under the guise of the emergency lead to various states creating new laws and changing existing laws pertaining to the regulation of the upcoming election.

President Trump's approach to the pandemic was classically conservative in that he did not nationalize the response, as called for by many liberal politicians and pundits who expected him to declare martial law and call out the army, but rather, acting within the purview of the US Constitution, Trump worked with the states to assist and to partner with them as they crafted their own responses based upon their own circumstances. This hands-off approach on the part of the president perhaps contributed to a somewhat laissez faire attitude regarding the growing phenomena of fiat changes to voting regulations on the state level including the papering of the house with unsolicited mail-in ballots, ballot harvesting, the weakening of standards for voter identification and the placement of voter drop boxes. While Trump gave lip service to stopping these practices, all of which were being done contrary to federal law and the constitution which delegates election law to elected state legislatures, not much was done on the federal level.

In retrospect, this lack of action on the part of the president might have been due to the stalling actions of deep state operatives embedded within his administration and this would probably include Attorney General Bill Barr. Indeed, it was revealed after the election that Attorney General Barr had known all along about an FBI investigation of Hunter Biden, and that he knew that the FBI had possession of the now infamous laptop with its massive amounts of incriminating evidence. Barr, who often opined publicly and eloquently on conservative values, had failed to reveal this information to the president or to the public. Had he done so, had he revealed the evidence of corruption on the part of Biden and his family, this revelation would have certainly adversely affected the Biden candidacy and, even more shocking, if Barr had revealed that the FBI was investigating Hunter Biden's interactions with Burisma Oil which would have scuttled the whole phony impeachment.

It could be argued that various laws regarding the election of 2020 might have appropriately been modified to comport with the COVID emergency but the legal means to make such laws resides with the state legislatures, elected to represent the public, and not with governors, state courts or unelected bureaucrats. Yet this is exactly what happened, laws were created without legislative debate and approval, and these unlawful actions had a particularly deleterious effect on the Trump campaign in the states that had been identified as the swing states, the states which would decide the national election. The changes in the laws, which in some cases were made in the days before and even in the days after the election, weakened the standards of identifying and verifying the voter and, as such, these laws clearly resulted in the proliferation of the fraud that took place.

Evidence suggests that the weakening of these standards of identification, the massive mailings of unsolicited ballots, the voter harvesting, the ending of signature verification, the drop boxes, the failure to purge the voter rolls of voters who had either passed away or who had moved out of state, the various questions raised regarding electronic voting associated with Smart Matic software and the Dominion voting machines, these factors, I argue, were all employed as tools in an overall, deliberate and coordinated conspiracy on the part of a number of interlocking figures, working in tandem, to steal the election from President Donald Trump by corrupting a few key states.

Much has been made by the detractors of these claims that voter fraud was rare and was, at any rate, not more pervasive this time around than it was during previous elections and this is probably true. Actual voter fraud, committed by an individual voter, is rare because such an act is a felony punishable by possible prison time. The issue at hand in the election of 2020 is not voter fraud per se but rather the issue is ballot fraud committed by either corrupt poll workers or by electronic means. Evidence suggests that such fraud did take place to a degree by which the election was stolen in the targeted states and that this conspiracy was supported, to varying degrees, by corrupt government officials, media, and state judges.

It should be noted, and it has been acknowledged by most of the liberal establishment, that no one expected President Trump to do as well with the voters as he did on election day. In spite of the massive rallies and the huge and emotional outpouring of support, the mainstream media and the pollsters continued onward with their dreary drumbeat of bad news and negativity perhaps operating under the assumption that such ongoing propaganda, which included rigged polls, would demoralize the Trump voter and thus suppress the vote. The conspirators were also depending on the big tech censorship which had learned lessons from their mistakes back in 2016 when they held a loose leash on free speech.

The Election of 2020

Election night was a surreal experience. Trump won early in Florida and shortly after he won in Texas and Ohio and he did so by substantial margins. Shortly before midnight, the so-called swing states of Georgia, Pennsylvania, Michigan, North Carolina and Wisconsin suddenly, and mysteriously, stopped counting. At the time of the shutdown, Trump was ahead in all of those states by comfortable margins. In Pennsylvania, at the time of the shutdown, Trump was ahead by over a half a million votes. For several hours following the shutdown the network commentators rambled on aimlessly trying to fill airtime. I remember going to bed at around 2 pm under the vague impression that Trump had won but with a strange feeling of unease over what I had observed.

The State of Arizona had been called for Biden by Fox News analyst Arnon Mishkin at 11:20 pm ET. There was no hard evidence at that time that Biden was ahead in Arizona as Mishkin, a Democrat who had voted for Hillary Clinton in 2016, made the call based upon mathematical analysis as opposed to any real and actual counting of the votes. We would later find out that much of the vote counting in general was conducted by data analysis and averaging as opposed to actual vote counting and this would also apply, according to controversial Attorney Sidney Powell and others, to the methodologies that would be employed in counting the votes by the Dominion voting machines that were used in over 20 states.

The early call by Fox News, a call that was not echoed by either CNN or MSNBC we should note, would subsequently cause Fox to precipitously drop in ratings and to lose a large swath of its conservative audience perhaps permanently. This news from Fox was reminiscent of when CBS Newsman Dan Rather called Florida for Gore in the election of 2000. Rather broadcasted this "news" on national television while sitting in front of a map of Florida colored in blue which I believe marked the beginning of what would become known as the red and blue states. We found out later that Gore was never ahead in Florida at any time and that Rather had launched his lie at a time when the polls had not yet closed in the western part of the Florida panhandle which was in a different time zone. In the same way that Rather's underhanded tactic contributed to the confusion in Florida and the delay of the 2000 election results, Mishkin's false announcement regarding Arizona was devastating to Trump and his false announcement arguably set the stage for the shutdown in the swing states which followed on its heels.

When questioned about the early call by Bret Baier the next day on Fox, Mishkin doubled down and, while not denying that fact that he had no hard evidence at the time of his call that Biden was ahead he stated: *We are not pulling back that call. There is vote, additional vote that will be reported in Maricopa County. We do not believe that this will change the tenor or the texture of the race, and we strongly believe that our call will stand. And that's why we're not pulling back the call.* (1.)

In other words, Mishkin lied when he declared on national television that Biden won Arizona under the assumption, and perhaps with the hope, that Biden would catch up later. Either way, Mishkin must have known that the early call would have a momentous effect in terms of sowing confusion and legitimizing the pauses in the counting, a situation that has never been adequately explained.

I would argue that the conspirators who sought to end the Trump presidency at any cost, those who had conspired against Trump from the very moment that he announced his candidacy for president at Trump Towers in 2015, did not expect the outpouring of support and the unprecedented numbers of votes that he would receive. Usually, as in the past, when one candidate or one party plotted to steal an election, the caper would be conducted only in a close race where the crime would more likely go undetected or it would be ignored. The conspirators against Trump, as was the case in 2020, did not expect Trump to do so well which is why, I would suggest, they had to take extraordinary measures in order to steal the election and, in the process, they had to depend upon the complete and seamless cooperation and loyalty of their friends who control the media, the means of communication. Like any coup, in order to ensure success, they had to seize control of the proverbial radio station and the microphone and this, for the Trump conspirators and haters, proved to be a proverbial piece of cake.

The fact is that President Trump increased his margins in every demographic except one which was white males. Trump did better in every major city including Chicago, New York, Los Angeles, San Francisco and even in my hometown of Boston. Trump won 18 of the 19 bellwether counties that have determined the election victor for decades, counties that voted for both Bush and Obama. Republicans won 28 of the 29 contested congressional races, added three state legislatures and did not lose a single house race. The only cities where Biden improved his margins over Hillary Clinton's 2016 margins were Philadelphia, Detroit, Atlanta and Milwaukee. Indeed, Biden's vote totals in those select cities, all situated in the swing states, were astronomical and, as such, went through the roof. Why did this happen in those cities?

On the Saturday before Election Day, Pennsylvania Attorney General Josh Shapiro tweeted that Trump was going to lose his state. The Pennsylvania Governor Tom Wolfe had changed election law without the constitutional benefit of a vote in the state legislature by declaring that votes would be counted up to three days after Election Day. Republicans responded by lodging a complaint with the Pennsylvania Supreme Court which ruled against them and allowed the law, passed by decree, to stand. Supreme Court Justice Samuel Alito would later step in and segregate those votes for a future ruling from the full Supreme Court, a ruling that the court would schedule for two days after the inauguration.

It was this issue in Pennsylvania, along with similar laws enacted without legislative debate or vote in Michigan, Georgia and Wisconsin and this issue formed the basis for Texas to file a complaint with the Supreme Court. The case brought by Texas against Pennsylvania was based upon the contention that by unconstitutionally changing their election laws, as Article II Section 2 of the US Constitution reserves the regulation of election law to the state legislatures, Pennsylvania, Georgia, Michigan and Wisconsin had violated the constitutional rights of the voters of Texas. The constitutional question puts aside the question as to whether such manipulation of the election laws in those states, outside of legislative authority, might have favored one candidate over another.

On December 8, The Supreme Court, in an unsigned opinion, declined to hear the case of Texas vs Pennsylvania, as filed by Texas Attorney General Tom Paxton. Texas had been supported with amicus briefs by over 100 Republican congressmen and by 10 state Attorney's General. The defending states were likewise joined by briefs from Attorney's General from 20 states. The Supreme Court claimed that the case lacked standing which many commentators found to be an odd position to take given that such lawsuits between states are exactly the appropriate venue for the Supreme Court.

One of the major problems associated with the claims that the election was stolen is the fact that over 50 lawsuits were filed, mostly filed by local citizens and by State officials who felt that their votes and the votes of their constituents had been suppressed for various reasons, and that none, with one exception, of these cases made it far enough into the system of jurisprudence as to allow for the presentation of the evidence which would have assumedly led to a rendering of judgement based upon its merits. Indeed, the rejection of these filings was used by the biased media, which regurgitated a Biden talking point, by falsely claiming that these technical dismissals proved that the Trump team had no evidence.

Hearings were held in Pennsylvania, Arizona and Georgia regarding voter fraud claims and the eye witness testimony emanating from those hearings was shocking. The media conspiracy generally either refused to cover these hearings or, if they did, they would mock and dismiss its participants. The Trump team had gathered hundreds of affidavits from witnesses to voter fraud and, we should note, an affidavit is sworn testimony given on the penalties of perjury and is, as such, the equivalent of testimony before a judge or before Congress. These affidavits testifying to voter fraud were rarely if ever investigated by the mainstream media which generally exhibited an alarming lack of interest. The media blackout added to an atmosphere of mistrust and this enhanced the sense that the media was effectively engaging in censorship. We should recall that during the campaign the media dismissed charges made against Hunter Biden and other members of the Biden family regarding influence peddling and kickbacks as these charges were denounced as Russian propaganda. NPR went so far as to openly state that they would simply not be covering the Hunter Biden story. Only after the election was the Hunter Biden story finally and mildly covered and this was only after Biden was assumed to be safely on his way to installation.

Whistleblowers came forward and they were in no way offered the respectful hearing that was received by the so-called whistleblower whose testimony was used as the foundation for the Trump impeachment. In that case the whistleblower admitted that he did not actually even hear the phone call between President Trump and Ukrainian Prime Minister Zelensky but was rather that he was operating on second-hand reports. To make matters worse, Rep. Adam Schiff entered a bogus transcript into the congressional record and had the nerve to describe his action, once uncovered, as a form of satire. To reveal the whistleblowers name publicly meant risking censorship as even US Senator Rand Paul was censored by big tech social media for merely mentioning his name in his official capacity as a Senator debating on the floor of the US Senate as part of a congressional hearing.

Whistleblowers who exposed voter fraud included Erie PA postman Richard Hopkins who claimed that his boss instructed postal workers to backdate ballots mailed after Election Day. Hopkins would later claim that he was coerced into recanting his testimony by federal agents. (2.) In Nevada, a state that was allegedly rife with ballot fraud emanating from Clark County, where Las Vegas is located, a whistleblower reported poll workers processing illegitimate ballots and non-poll workers forming a "human wall" near a Biden/Harris van to block the view of individuals filling out what the whistleblower believed to have been ballots. (3.) Phil Kline, former Kansas Attorney General and Attorney with the Thomas Moore Society Amistad Project, claimed in a press conference that he had eye witness evidence that 130,000 to 280,000 completed ballots were shipped by truck from Bethpage New York to Lancaster Pennsylvania where they disappeared two days before the election. (4.)

Former New York City Mayor Rudolph Giuliani, serving as head of the Trump campaign legal team, filed a lawsuit claiming that 900,000 illegal ballots were cast in Pennsylvania. Claiming that the Pennsylvania election was a "disaster," Giuliani claimed that he had evidence of people being harassed at polling places and that Republican observers were kept out of the counting areas for a 24-hour period while 135,000 mail-in ballots were counted. Giuliani claimed that he had upwards of 50 observers who claimed that they were kept more than six feet away from the counting. I will reiterate that the problem here, as I see it, is that this evidence was not presented in a courtroom, the appropriate venue for such criminal accusations, because no judge allowed the evidence to get to that point. (5.)

 Wayne County, Michigan, where Detroit is located, was a particularly egregious case regarding ballot fraud allegations with its Democratic Party machine and its long-standing reputation for corruption. Legitimate charges of fraud had been made in Detroit over several decades including after the election of 2012. Green Party presidential candidate Jill Stein called for a recount in 2016 which was suspended after evidence of voter fraud began to emerge and the corrupt machine was threatened with exposure. This time around there were multiple affidavits from witnesses who claimed to have seen such shady events as white vans pulling up to the loading dock behind the TCF Center at around 4 o clock in the morning where pallets of pristine ballots were unloaded and then fed into voting machines. The day after the election, the counting continued with observers denied access and where empty pizza boxes were taped to the windows of the TCF Center to prevent viewing from the outside. Among the many who testified in Detroit, Van Buren County Treasurer Trisha Nesbitt, who volunteered as a poll challenger at the TCF Center, testified to harassment and shady dealings as she tried to fulfill her work. (6.) Barry Doherty submitted an affidavit as a witness to ballot fraud in Detroit where he described seeing online networked voting machines. (7.)

The 2020 election should be studied by College students majoring in Data Analytics, but I would not expect this to happen on a large-scale any time soon. Virginia Data Scientist Sarah Eaglesfield was tracking the vote count in real time when she noticed a glitch. She observed that from 5:07 to 5:12 am her state lost 169,000 votes. Up until that time, Trump had been consistently ahead. (8.) Award winning journalist Jim Hoft from Gateway Pundit, who has done a great job reporting ballot irregularities, reported data analysis which speculated that millions of votes from all of the states that used Dominion voting machines were either switched from Trump to Biden or were erased from the Trump column. This analysis specifically points to Rock County, Wisconsin with the claim that 9,514 votes there were switched from Trump to Biden. (9.) These are sensational and astonishing charges which deserve follow-up from the mainstream media. Instead, these stories were either ignored or they were mocked with the usual accusation, one that allows for a convenient dismissal, which is that these stories were nothing more than made up conspiracy theories.

Data analysis posted on MIL-OPS, a Defense Department website serving military officers sites Benford's Law, or the 1st digit law to demonstrate that analysis of the vote from Chicago, Milwaukee and Pittsburgh indicate fraud that benefited Biden. Benford's law analysis has been used in federal, state and local court and was used to analyze voter fraud in the 2000 and 2004 elections. This analysis raised questions about Wednesday morning ballot drops in Michigan and Wisconsin where Republicans had previously outpaced Democrats in both states in terms of mail-in ballot requests and returns, and yet, the drops overwhelmingly were tallied for Biden. (10.)

A case involving felony charges was brought against Kelly Reagan Brunner, a Texas social worker, who was charged with fraudulently filling out 67 ballots in the name of patients with intellectual and developmental disabilities living in the Mexia State Supported Living Center without their knowledge. (11.) Similar reports of like nature emanated out of Wisconsin including ballots that were cast by nursing home workers in the name of elderly and disabled patients without their consent or those who had passed away before election day. While this type of fraud, along with several cases where upwards of thousands of ballots were reportedly cast from homeless shelters in Georgia and in the name of homeless people registered in California, no doubt has occurred in the past, this election witnessed unprecedented levels of this type of fraud.

The most sensational and controversial charges of ballot fraud were rendered by Georgia Attorney Linn Wood and Attorney Sidney Powell who is now being threatened with a law-suit by Dominion Voting Machines. Powell filed lawsuits, which she described as the Kraken, against Georgia, Michigan, Wisconsin and elsewhere but, as would be the case with all of the lawsuits filed by the Trump team and by the various Trump supporters, her cases have either been dismissed on technicalities or they were shelved which means that her evidence has yet to be aired, adjudicated and vetted.

Powell, who has challenged Dominion to sue her so she could get them under oath as part of discovery, has charged that Dominion was created with Venezuelan money for the purpose of rigging elections for Hugo Chavez. Powell claims that the voting machines were online and, as such, "people could remotely watch the votes and flip them in real time." Powell claims: "We have evidence now of information from the systems going to three or four different foreign countries during the time of the election, those countries themselves could have watched the live votes come in and changed the numbers. There's significant evidence of foreign interference from the worst communist countries on the Earth with our election." (12.)

To not cover the charges made by Linn Wood and Sidney Powell would render this entire narrative incomplete since her charges played such a prominent public role in the narrative. I shall thus forge forward with such coverage with the acknowledgement and disclaimer that I have no firsthand knowledge regarding the veracity of these charges, and I do not, as such, endorse these views. Besides the Dominion work, Powell claimed, among other things, that she had identified 450,000 ballots that contain only a single vote for Joe Biden and no other candidate.

The Dominion-Smartmatic story first emerged as a public question when it was discovered that the 22 Dominion voting machines used in Antrim County, Michigan had flipped 6,000 Trump votes to Biden and that these machines had also flipped votes away from local candidates and a local ballot initiative. The glitch, which was described as such by most media, once discovered, was claimed to have been a human error and the votes were then switched back to the rightful candidates. A subsequent forensic audit of the machines, ordered by a local judge, proved to be controversial and both sides claimed that they were right. Either way, we should note that 47 other counties in Michigan also use the suspect Dominion software as do over 20 states including Georgia and Arizona. It also appears that virtually all of the voting errors, the so-called glitches, whether resulting from rigged machines or from human error, when discovered, would invariably favor Biden.

Much more has been documented elsewhere regarding this sad and sordid tale and, hopefully, much more will be written. Suffice to say that the story is not over as, indeed, the story is just beginning. We must demand that this issue be vetted and let the chops fall where they may. Anything less would be too compromising for our freedoms and for our future as a free people living in a free nation.

The US Capitol is breached

I waited with bated breath for Wednesday, January 6, 2021 as I viewed this date as the last opportunity for the ballot fraud evidence to be publicly presented and vetted. Seven states had nominated alternative Republican delegations of electors who would challenge the Biden delegations that had been certified by governors in those seven states. This represented the beginning, although extremely late in the day and much too late for this election, of state legislatures asserting their constitutional prerogative to ratify electors. The six states to nominate alternative delegations which would contest their respective elections on January 6th were Georgia, Pennsylvania, Michigan, Wisconsin, Nevada and Arizona. Trump was winning in all of these on election night before the counting was stopped and all of them would later switch to Biden, with thin margins, after a process that stretched out over days and weeks in a process that was fraught with opportunity for fraud. The six states were joined by New Mexico which voted for Biden on election night but where apparently the Republican Party sought to present evidence of fraud.

In order for a state to contest their election and challenge their official delegation of electors, one house member would have to be joined by one Senator who would then jointly challenge, in writing, the election in that state. The Vice President of the United States, acting in the capacity as President of the joint session of Congress, would then be triggered to call for a debate which could go on for up to two hours. Congressman Mo Brooks of Alabama stepped forward early to announce that he would challenge all of the states that were sending alternative delegations and he was soon joined by Senator Josh Hawley of Missouri. Brooks would soon be joined by over 140 representatives and Hawley by 12 Senators.

With 7 staters in contention, and with each receiving two hours to debate their evidence, the electoral count was expected to drag on for several days. Many scholars pointed to a legal theory that held that Vice President Pence, as president of the assembly, had plenary powers, or absolute authority to accept, reject, or ignore the credentials of the delegates. If Pence rejected or ignored the delegation from at least 2 states than neither candidate would have enough delegates to be elected as president. If this scenario were to play out, a special session of Congress would be convened with each state sending a single delegate to vote for president. Since the delegate would be chosen, as the constitution requires, by the respective state legislatures, and given that fact that there are at least 21 state legislatures with Republican majorities, than in this scenario Trump would win the presidency.

While Trump publicly and assumedly privately pressured Mike Pence to go that route, Pence rejected that course of action. Either way, Pence was prepared to fulfill his constitutional responsibility to call for a debate once a state election was properly contested and he was scheduled to call each delegation in alphabetical order with Arizona first up as a contested state. I watched the drama as Arizona was called, I watched as the debate began and as the stunning evidence began to be rolled out.

Then, all of a sudden, something strange and unexpected happened.

Protesters surged into the Capitol, the hearings were suspended, and, in the wee hours of the night, Congress would stealthily re-convene and would proceed to push through the Biden nomination without opposition. Thus, the evidence of ballot fraud would be successfully suppressed, and the lie would be forever sealed.

Suddenly the focus was on the protesters outside the Capitol who were pushing their way in. It should be noted that regardless of whether the protesters were Trump supporters or whether they were Antifa disguised as Trump supporters, and there were numerous rumors and reports indicating that this would happen in the days leading up to the protest, the vast majority of the hundreds of thousands of protesters were peaceful families simply, and I may add joyfully, demonstrating their free speech opposition to what over half of Republicans and a large share of Democrats believe to be a stolen election.

I watched most of Trump's speech to the protesters and I did not hear anything remotely indicating incitement or any call for violence. In fact, at least the portion of his speech that I heard was a rather hum-drum recanting of his many accomplishments as president. There was no evidence, nor will any emerge to indicate that Trump sought to do anything other than lend support to the peaceful protesters. There was no way of knowing that a small group of rowdies would breach the Capitol and, we should note, unlike the leftist shock troops who had been looting predominantly black businesses, burning predominantly black neighborhoods and murdering black people, including children, in cities across America during the months leading up to the election, those who breached the Capitol, while wrong and while trespassing, were nevertheless peaceful and they did not damage property other than a few broken windows. It should also be noted that leftists, going back to the Bush Administration with occupations by Code Pink and during the Brett Kavanaugh nomination to the Supreme Court, had occupied areas of the Capitol complex.

Whether or not the Capitol breach was a planned operation or whether it was a spontaneous action by over rambunctious Trump supporters, Trump's enemies, those who opposed him from the moment he got off the escalator at Trump Tower, those who had engaged in an unrelenting agenda of propaganda and lies every day since, naturally seized on the opportunity to turn up the heat on both Trump and his 75 million followers. Putting aside the fact that they had supported insurrection, terror, and violence for the preceding months in cities across America, now, by hyping up the Capitol breach, Trump, and by extension his supporters, were to be smeared as insurrectionist terrorists. Now Trump, anyone supporting Trump and anyone questioning the legitimacy of the election would risk being called a terrorist.

As this short pamphlet goes to press, President Trump is facing another phony impeachment with one week left in office.

We are all Socialists Now

I have included in this book, in the appendix, a copy of President Trump's extraordinary inaugural address. This speech, which should be read by and should be discussed by every American high school student and every student of the US Constitution, should be viewed as a blueprint for patriots going forward, especially in these perilous times.

In the speech, President Trump noted the following:

...we are not merely transferring power from one administration to another or from one party to another, but we are transferring power from Washington, DC, and giving it back to you, the people.

We should keep in mind that Donald Trump was not prone to delivering the usual flowery speech filled with sophistries, double-talk and innuendo, the type that we have come to expect from politicians from both political parties. Whether we like his style or not, we should agree that President Trump is known for his bluntness and simple honesty, that Trump says what he means and he means what he says.

Trump's enemies tried to make hay out of their claim that Trump lied and, technically, if put under a microscope, this was true. We should note that the type of lies, or exaggerations, or embellishments that Trump engaged in were the type of tall tales or fibs, what Mark Twain called a stretcher, that a person might tell at a Thanksgiving dinner where they might exaggerate over the size of the fish they caught. Trump might occasionally fib over such things as the size of the crowd at his inauguration. While I hold this against him, and while I would suggest that this type of thing was unnecessary for him as the truth of his life and his activities are big enough to render such tendencies as a bit boorish. When it came to things that really mattered, however, things that were real, Trump tended to be brutally honest.

Trump's tall tales were, as such, harmless exaggerations. This would contrast well with the great lies of history such as when President Barack Obama went around the country promoting Obamacare by declaring *If you like your healthcare plan, you can keep your healthcare plan…if you like your doctor, you can keep your doctor.* Or, even worse, The Gulf of Tonkin Resolution, based on a fabrication, that drew the United States into the Vietnam War or lies told previously by Presidents Franklin D. Roosevelt and Woodrow Wilson in terms of promises to not get the United States embroiled into World Wars 1 and II.

Indeed, as is so often the case with the left, their complaints about Trump's fibs was an inversion and a psychological projection as it was not his white lies that they were concerned about but, rather, they were concerned about his truth telling in the real sense. This is why, now that they have successfully enacted their coup, the first thing they are trying to do, as they feel emboldened and intoxicated with their newly seized powers, is to silence Trump by having him censored from Twitter and this, I fear, is just the beginning for Trump and, by extension, for the rest of us.

When President Trump spoke of transferring power from Washington D.C., which he would accurately describe as the swamp, he meant business and this, more than anything, was the source of the hatred that would be directed against him. Trump, thus, intended to begin the process of dismantling the colossal behemoth of the informal, unelected, bureaucratic, increasingly internationalist administrative state that had been enthroned with the 1912 election of Woodrow Wilson. The fascinating history of this enthronement, which is worth studying, is beyond the scope of this brief treatise. Suffice to say that the enthronement of the socialistic administrative state was advanced by such events as the creation of the Federal Reserve system, the implementation of the income tax, emergency legislation enacted by FDR in response to the depression and the formalization of the national security apparatus implemented by executive orders of President Harry S. Truman.

With the possible exception of President John F. Kennedy, and we know, unfortunately, what happened to him, Trump was the only president in recent times to take on this establishment that seeks to transfer the sovereign constitutional rights of the citizen, under God, to itself. The election steal represents a return of those powers from the people, under the constitution, back to what Trump accurately referred to as the deep state. History will tell as to whether we are living through a time by which the deep state will consolidate its powers by leaving the rest of us in a condition where rights are granted as privileges at the whim of an invisible elite or, hopefully, this is the last gasp, the last desperate grab for power, by a deep state that is confronting a growing consciousness on the part of the people who are becoming aware of their own natural and sovereign rights under God.

Pearl Harbor invasion plotter, Japanese Admiral Isoroku Yamamoto, reportedly wrote in his diary: *I fear all we have done is to awaken a sleeping giant and fill him with a terrible resolve.*

Solutions

As the old saying goes, when God closes a door, he opens a window, and this aphorism applies to our stolen election. We should step back, reflect on what we have learned, and figure out how to move forward. Firstly, let me state for the record, that whoever is inaugurated on January 20th, 2021, that person will be the President of the United States and that person will be, as such, my president. We must not sink to the level of the anti-American Trump haters who denied that Donald Trump was the president, and in that case, there was no controversy regarding his election, with the bumper sticker slogan "he's not my president."

 The first issue before us, one that must be addressed if we are to ever expect another free election anywhere in the United States, is to advocate for comprehensive election reform. This, firstly, means that we must insist upon a continuation of the documentation of the evidence that the election was stolen. We must support and encourage those who continue to gather the evidence and we must continue to encourage our friends, as well as our foes, in the media to research and to investigate this question. We must insist that the final and complete vote is counted, categorized and publicized in every state.

Following are some recommendations:

1. We must demand that the Dominion voting machines, the Smartmatic software and all electronic voting machines be discarded and are never used again. Most other nations and more than half of our states do not use electronic voting machines. They count the ballots the old-fashioned way, they do it by hand.

2. We must insure that the counting of ballots is conducted in the open with monitors from both parties at the counting table at all times. There were too many examples during this election of Republicans shut out of the process, particularly in Atlanta, Philadelphia, Detroit and Phoenix. Even third world dictatorships do this. I

seem to recall how former President Jimmy Carter was celebrated for his missions, as part of the Carter Institute, to various countries accompanied by teams of monitors during elections. The fact that Americans were prevented from observing the counting of ballots in certain precincts constitutes perhaps the biggest and most disgraceful scandal to emerge in what was otherwise and easily the most corrupt election in American history.

3. We must institute a system of voter ID in all fifty states. If we can have enhanced drivers licenses, we should be able to implement a voter ID system that would be made available for free to all qualified citizens of the United States. Such systems have been often denounced as racist by such phony groups as the Brennan Center for Justice, a George Soros backed AstroTurf organization that pushed this piece of propaganda as a means of preventing voter registration. Voter ID should be made easy and it should be free.

4. We must insist that our states, our counties and our local precincts purge their voter rolls of people who have either passed away, are registered but are underage, are unqualified for various reasons, or who have moved out of the county or state. This could be done simply by contacting and confirming each registered voter whose name appears on the voter roll. Too many votes have been cast by corrupt clerks and poll workers, especially during this election, after the polls have closed and when they check to rolls to see which registered voter did not vote so they can proceed to cast a fraudulent vote.

Such practices are common in certain corrupt cities. Former MSNBC commentator Chris Matthews explained how this works during his program, Hardball, in 2011:

People call up, see if you voted or you're not going to vote. Then all of a sudden somebody does come and vote for you. This is an old strategy in big-city politics. . . . I know all about it in North Philly — it's what went on, and I believe it still goes on.

The election fraud raised an awareness on the part of state legislatures in the corrupted states, and of state legislatures in general, regarding their constitutional responsibilities. Never again should we tolerate the usurpation of their constitutional prerogative, which had in this election been usurped by corrupt Governors, state Secretaries of State, state judges and other various unelected bureaucrats, to arbitrarily invent election laws. One way to reform this process, and a way to promote that more overall sovereign powers return to their rightful place, the elected assemblies of the people of the state, would be for citizens to run for these offices.

If you are retired, a housewife, an empty nester, a teenager, or if you simply have the time, you could run for state rep or state senator and you could win with extraordinarily little money or name recognition. There are many tools that are available, are free, and are at your disposal including social media, cable TV, local political clubs, and local press.

Even if you do not win, by running, you will receive media coverage and you will, as such, have the opportunity to be heard and to get an issue or two over the plate. Most state districts are small enough that you could go door to door of have a few coffee klatches to meet voters and gather signatures. Indeed, this should be viewed as a civic exercise and, besides, it is an extremely rewarding personal experience.

Freedom doesn't grow on trees. We must exercise the levers of freedom or they will wither. In the same way that we are responsible for the direction of our own lives and our own destiny, and that of our families, we are responsible for preserving, protecting and defending our communities, our states and our nations.

It is time for the sleeping giant to wake up!

Appendix

Donald Trump Inaugural Address – January 20, 2017

We, the citizens of America, are now joined in a great national effort to rebuild our country and restore its promise for all of our people. Together, we will determine the course of America and the world for many, many years to come.

We will face challenges. We will confront hardships, but we will get the job done. Every four years, we gather on these steps to carry out the orderly and peaceful transfer of power. And we are grateful to President Obama and first lady Michelle Obama for their gracious aid throughout this transition. They have been magnificent. Thank you.

Today's ceremony, however, has very special meaning, because today, we are not merely transferring power from one administration to another or from one party to another, but we are transferring power from Washington, DC, and giving it back to you, the people.

For too long, [those in politics] have reaped the rewards of government while people have borne the cost. Washington flourished, but the people did not share in its wealth.

Politicians prospered, but the jobs left, and the factories closed. The establishment protected itself, but not the citizens of our country. Their victories have not been your victories. Their triumphs have not been your triumphs and while they celebrated in our nation's capital, there was little to celebrate for struggling families all across our land.

That all changes starting right here and right now because this moment is your moment. It belongs to you. It belongs to everyone gathered here today and everyone watching all across America. This is your day. This is your celebration. And this, the United States of America, is your country.

Because what truly matters is not what truly controls our government but whether our government is controlled by the people. January 20, 2017 will be remembered as the day the people became the rulers of this nation again.

The forgotten men and women of our country will be forgotten no longer. Everyone is listening to you now. You came by the tens of millions to become part of a historic movement, the likes of which the world has never seen before.

At the center of this movement is a crucial conviction, that a nation exists to serve its citizens. Americans want great schools for their children, safe neighborhoods for their families, and good jobs for themselves. These are just and reasonable demands of righteous people and a righteous public. But for too many of our citizens, a different reality exists.

Mothers and children trapped in poverty in our inner cities, rusted-out factories, scattered like tombstones across the landscape of our nation, an education system flush with cash but which leaves our young and beautiful students deprived of all knowledge.

And the crime and the gangs and the drugs that have stolen too many lives and robbed our country of so much unrealized potential. This American carnage stops right here and stops right now.

For many decades, we have enriched foreign industry at the expense of American industry, subsidized the armies of other countries while allowing for the very sad depletion of our military.

We have defended other nations' borders while refusing to defend our own and spend trillions and trillions of dollars overseas while America's infrastructure has fallen into disrepair and decay.

We've made other countries rich while the wealth, strength, and confidence of our country has dissipated over the horizon. One by one, the factories shuttered and left our shores with not even a thought about the millions and millions of American workers that were left behind. The wealth of our middle class has been ripped from their homes and then redistributed all across the world.

But that is the past, and now we are looking only to the future. We assembled here today are issuing a new decree to be heard in every city, in every foreign capital and in every hall of power. From this day forward, a new vision will govern our land. From this day forward, it's going to be only America first, America first.

Every decision on trade, on taxes, on immigration, on foreign affairs will be made to benefit American workers and American families. We must protect our borders from the ravages of other countries making our products, stealing our companies, and destroying our jobs.

Protection will lead to great prosperity and strength. I will fight for you with every breath in my body. And I will never ever let you down.

America will start winning again, winning like never before. We will bring back our jobs. We will bring back our borders. We will bring back our wealth. And we will bring back our dreams. We will build new roads and highways and bridges and airports and tunnels and railways all across our wonderful nation. We will get our people off of welfare and back to work, rebuilding our country with American hands and American labor.

We will follow two simple rules: Buy American and hire American.

We will seek friendship and goodwill with the nations of the world, but we do so with the understanding that it is the right of all nations to put their own interests first. We do not seek to impose our way of life on anyone, but rather to let it shine as an example. We will shine for everyone to follow. We will reinforce old alliances and form new ones and reform the world against radical Islamic terrorism, which we will eradicate from the face of the Earth.

At the bedrock of our politics will be a total allegiance to the United States of America and through our loyalty to our country, we will rediscover our loyalty to each other. When you open your heart to patriotism, there is no room for prejudice. The Bible tells us how good and pleasant it is when God's people live together in unity. We must speak our minds openly, debate our disagreements honestly, but always pursue solidarity.

When America is united, America is totally unstoppable.

There should be no fear. We are protected, and we will always be protected. We will be protected by the great men and women of our military and law enforcement. And most importantly, we will be protected by God.

Finally, we must think big and dream even bigger. In America, we understand that a nation is only living as long it is striving. We will no longer accept politicians who are all talk and no action, constantly complaining but never doing anything about it. The time for empty talk is over.

Now arrives the hour of action. Do not allow anyone to tell you that it cannot be done. No challenge can match the heart and fight and spirit of America. We will not fail. Our country will thrive and prosper again. We stand at the birth of a new millennium, ready to unlock the mysteries of space, to free the Earth from the miseries of disease and harness the energies, industries and technologies of tomorrow.

A new national pride will stir ourselves, lift our sights, and heal our divisions. It's time to remember that old wisdom our soldiers will never forget, that whether we are black or brown or white, we all bleed the same red blood of patriots. We all enjoy the same glorious freedoms. And we all salute the same great American flag.

And whether a child is born in the urban sprawl of Detroit or the wind-swept plains of Nebraska, they look at the same night sky. They fill their heart with the same dreams, and they are infused with the breath of life by the same almighty creator.

So, to all Americans, in every city near and far, small and large, from mountain to mountain, from ocean to ocean, hear these words: you will never be ignored again.

Your voice, your hopes, and your dreams will define our American destiny. And your courage, goodness, and love will forever guide us along the way.

Together, we will make America strong again. We will make America wealthy again. We will make America proud again. We will make America safe again.

And yes, together, we will make America great again.

Thank you. God bless you. And God bless America.

Notes

1. Los Angeles Times: Why Fox News analyst Arnon Mishkin called Arizona for Biden on election night. Nov. 5, 2020

2. Business Insider: Video shows USPS "whistleblower" was not alone when swearing to affidavit alleging mail-in ballot fraud. Nov. 15, 2020

3. Breitbart: Nevada Whistleblower: Workers Instructed to Process Illegitimate Ballots, Hannah Bleau, Nov. 9, 2020

4. WBAP News Talk: Law Firm Claims More Than 280K Pre-marked Ballots Disappeared in Pennsylvania

5. Washington Examiner: Rudy Giuliani: Trump campaign has enough evidence to change Pennsylvania election results. Anthony Leonardi, Nov. 8, 2020

6. The Federalist: First-Hand Account of Election Fraud in Detroit: "They did not want us to see what was happening, John Daniel Davidson, Nov. 6, 2020

7. YouTube Interview: Barry Doherty describes Wi-Fi Networks, Boxes of empty ballots, Networked voting machines.

8. Gateway Pundit: Captured in Real Time: That Moment in Virginia at 5:12 AM Where they Took 373,000 Votes Off the State Totals Jim Hoft, Nov. 9, 2020

9. Gateway Pundit: Analysis of Election Night Data from All States Shows MILLIONS OF VOTES Either Switched from President Trump to Biden or Were Lost — Using Dominion and Other Systems Jim Hoft, Nov. 10, 2020

10. Geller Report: Overall Multi-State Data: Mathematical Evidence, Pamela Geller, Nov. 8, 2020

11. Daily Wire: Texas Charges Social Worker With 134 Felony Counts Involving Election Fraud, Ryan Saavedra, Nov. 6, 2020

12. The Epoch Times, Sidney Powell: Trump Team will prove case within the next two weeks in court. Jack Phillips, Nov. 20, 2020

13. National Review, Media are Flat Wrong to dismiss voter fraud Concerns. John Fund, August 15, 2015

www.ingramcontent.com/pod-product-compliance
Lightning Source LLC
Chambersburg PA
CBHW050756250726
48662CB00005B/2240